Winter Song

A Poem by William Shakespeare

Illustrated by Melanie Hall

Introduction by Alice Provensen

WORDSONG

Honesdale, Pennsylvania

The artist wishes to thank Deborah Curran-Aquino, Ph.D., and Drea Leed
for sharing their knowledge of Shakespeare and the Elizabethan era.

Wordsong
An Imprint of Boyds Mills Press, Inc.
A Highlights Company
815 Church Street
Honesdale, Pennsylvania 18431
Printed in China

Library of Congress Cataloging-in-Publication Data

Shakespeare, William, 1564–1616.
Winter song / by William Shakespeare ; illustrated by Melanie Hall.— 1st ed.
p. cm.
ISBN-13: 978-1-59078-275-0 (hardcover : alk. paper)
1. Winter—Juvenile poetry. 2. Children's poetry, English. I. Hall, Melanie W. II. Title.

PR2842.H36 2006
821.3'3—dc22

2006000760

First edition, 2006
The text of this book is set in Bernhard Roman.
The illustrations are done in mixed media.
Visit our Web site at www.boydsmillspress.com

10 9 8 7 6 5 4 3 2 1

To my mother, Doris Goldfield Winsten, with love always
—M. H.

Introduction

William Shakespeare lived over four hundred years ago (1564–1616) and is considered the finest writer in the English language.

"Winter Song," the poem illustrated in this book, is from his romantic comedy *Love's Labor's Lost*. It depicts winter in Shakespeare's time, but its imagery is just as appropriate today. Like crisp, new-fallen snow, Shakespeare's descriptions are as appealing now as they were in sixteenth-century England. The red noses and frozen toes of young snowballers were the same for children of Shakespeare's time as they are for present-day kids. After chilly outdoor play, the pleasure of hot treats in a warm kitchen is still a universal delight.

Poetry has always played an important role in people's lives. In former times, poetry was usually read aloud. In fact, Shakespeare wrote his work to be spoken. So read his poem aloud to yourself or to your family and friends. As you do, see how the illustrations help you imagine Shakespeare's wintry world. Sit by your fireside or at your kitchen table, with hot cocoa and cookies, and enjoy.

—*Alice Provensen*

When icicles

hang by the wall,

And Dick
the shepherd
blows his nail,

And Tom bears logs
into the hall,

And milk comes
frozen home in pail,

When blood is nipped,
and ways be foul,

Then nightly sings
the staring owl,
Tu-who;
Tu-whit, tu-who:
a merry note,

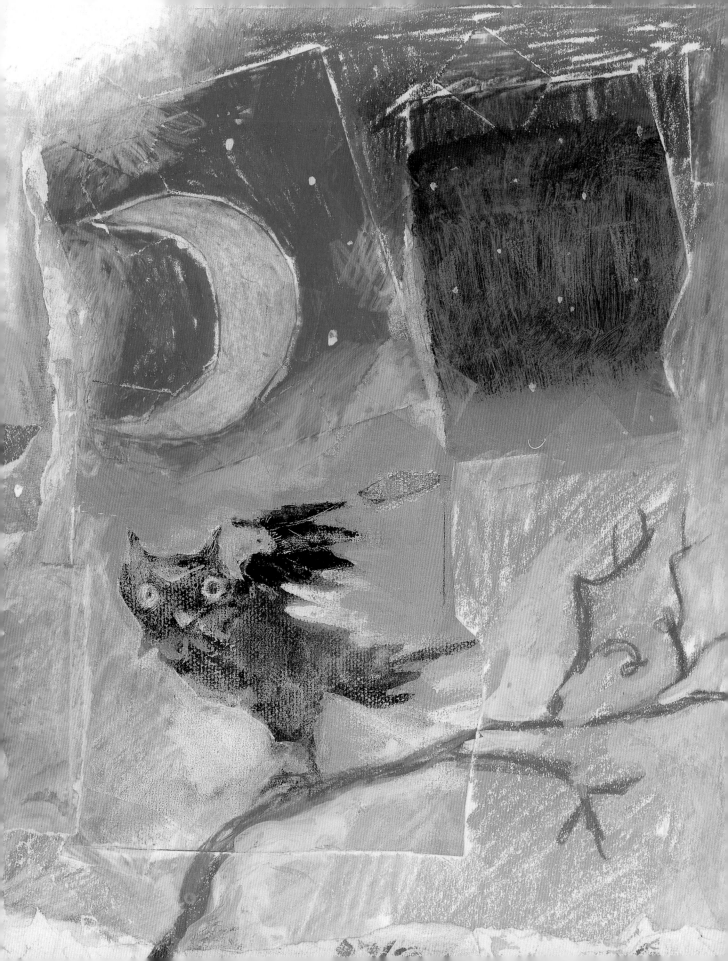

While greasy Joan

doth keel the pot.

When all aloud
the wind doth blow,
And coughing
drowns the
parson's saw,

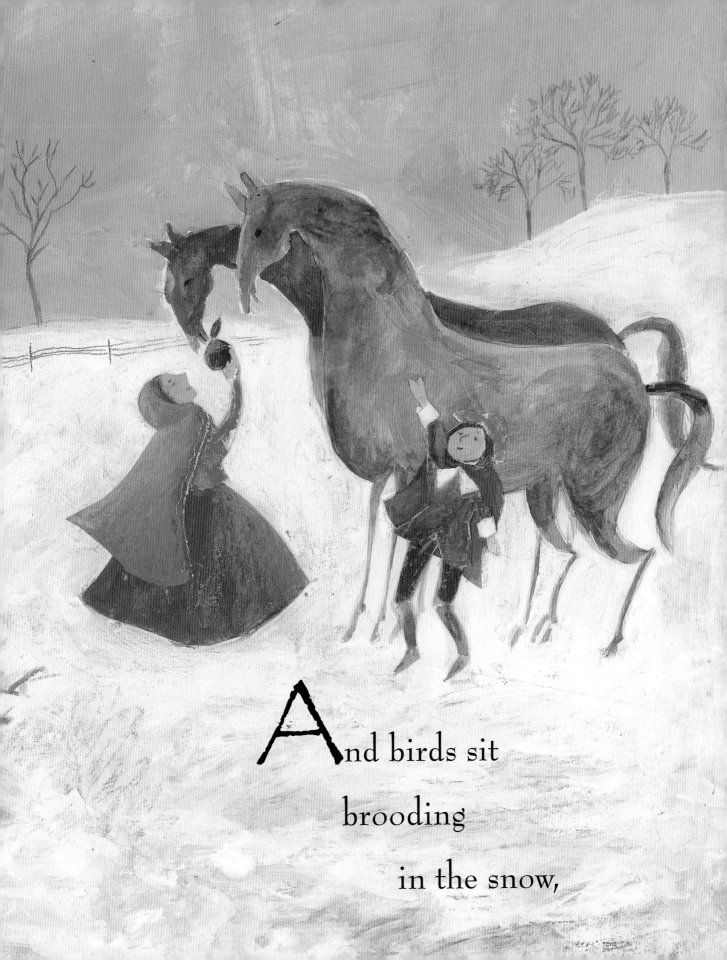

And birds sit brooding in the snow,

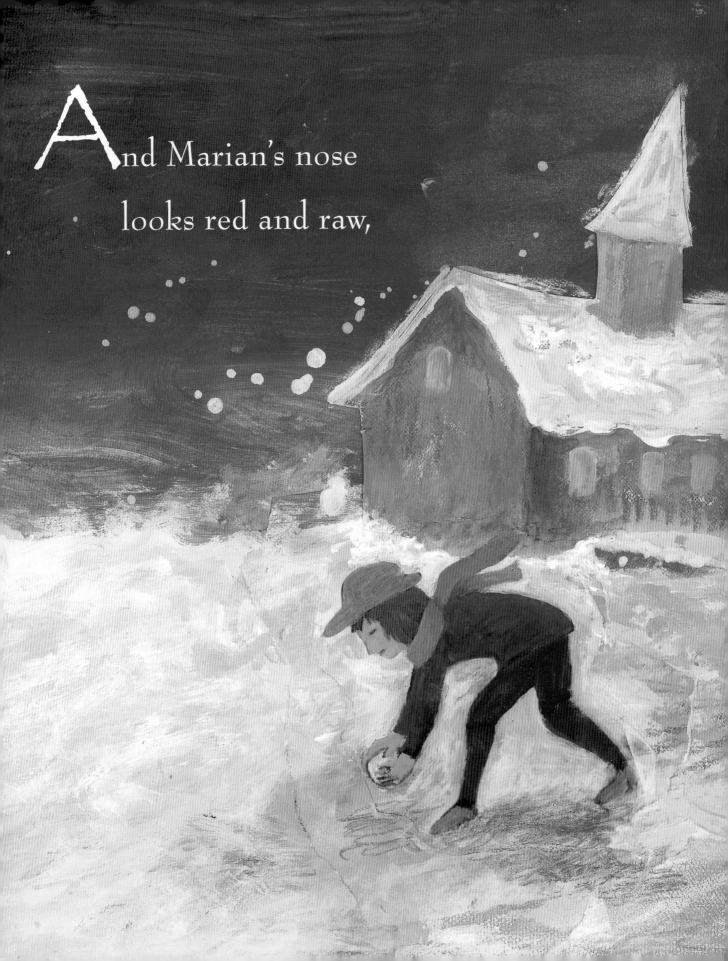

And Marian's nose
looks red and raw,

When roasted crabs
hiss in the bowl,

Then nightly sings
the staring owl,
Tu-who;
Tu-whit, tu-who:
a merry note,

While greasy Joan
doth keel the pot.

Glossary

blows his nail: blows on fingernails, to warm fingers and hand

when blood is nipped: painfully cold

ways be foul: when roads are muddy

doth: does

keel the pot: to cool the pot by stirring, to keep it from boiling over

parson's saw: the parson's sermon

birds sit brooding in the snow: birds sitting like hens do on their eggs

roasted crabs hiss in the bowl: roasted crab apples floating in a punch bowl full of ale or cider